Training Exercises

Training Exercises
Danny Hayward

What hath night to do with sleep
Tis only daylight which makes sin

There are beautiful ways of trimming a hedge

Anti-purge

Letter to Dom Hale

Five Reports

Anti-purge

No but Genoa

(Keston Sutherland)[1]

In 'poiesis', writes the medieval historian Johann Huizinga, 'things have a different physiognomy from the one they wear in "ordinary life", and are bound by ties other than logic and causality'.[2] This is a conventional definition of poetics, presented in a book about 'play', by an author interested in the traditions of popular festivities.

In the 2003 film 'Get Rid of Yourself', the uptown NY art-fashion collective Bernadette Corporation present a gloss on this idea of 'poiesis', this time in the words of an anarchist present during the anti-G8 riots that took place in Genoa in July 2001. The script is read by the actor Chloë Sevigny, playing the anarchist, who is herself watching a friend destroying an ATM with a hammer:

> She spent like ten, fifteen minutes destroying the ATM screen.
> She looked crazy. She looked happy.
> It was a kind of joyful insanity.[3]

This is not a metaphor for Huizinga's generalities so much as its exact generic equivalent. The Italian ATM machine is Huizinga's 'logic and causality', its smashed up screen his 'new physiognomy', the joyful insanity of the protestor the drunken licentiousness of the medieval festival from which the medieval historian derives his material, the Brueghelian game, the period of licensed indulgence in which all hierarchies have been turned upside down. 'The poet says "speech thorn" for "tongue"', says Huizinga, '"floor of the hall of the winds" for "earth", "tree wolf" for "wind" etc.'.[4] 'He is setting his hearers poetic riddles which are being tacitly solved'.[5] The emphasis on the brief duration of this act of criminal vandalism – like ten, fifteen minutes – is itself analogical material, this time for the representative window in which the rules of 'ordinary life' can be suspended, and so an acknowledgement that in order for the experience of poiesis to be real, it must itself be subject to the laws of social gravity: the duration of the festivities which define the amount of time in which it is possible to exist before the ordinary imperatives (including the imperatives of the stomach) reassert themselves. The point of the festivities is to turn ordinary feeling upside down; but it is also to acknowledge that it may no longer be useful to talk about how you 'really do' think, argue, or feel, and also to accept that in order to say or understand something new, it is sometimes necessary to lie, just as in certain situations it might be necessary to lie to participate in a game.

'Poiesis' is the liberation of things from the physiognomies that they ordinarily wear. The destruction of the ATM is a poetic act, the simplest imaginable, a perfect abstract negation, producing nothing. In Bernadette Corporation's film it is, additionally, a means for 'getting rid of yourself', an act of negation performed on an object that switches into an act of transformation performed on the self, a 'poetic' self-overcoming in which no one has to reveal or disclose or confess anything about themselves at all, but whose result is nevertheless a subjective poetic experience: 'insane joy'. I want to talk here for perhaps ten or fifteen minutes about this act of negation, which is to say, in the Situationist jargon on which the Bernadette Corporation themselves draw, not about the poetics of getting rid of yourself, but about getting rid of yourself *as* poetry.

A word by way of introduction: the essays and texts in this compilation grew out of my increasing dependency on poetry. The main idea that keeps coming back in them is that saying what I don't mean is one way of keeping myself alive. I am still learning (perhaps I will never really learn) to know what it means to decline to say whether I actually mean this; or to say different things in different places and to mean all of them; or basically to be a 'lyric poet', an incoherent concatenation of incoherent moods, including in what I have to say about poetry itself. The absurdity or plausible deniability of the argument of this first text is a reflection of my own resistance to it; a toy argument, made out of toy objects. Do I mean this. Transformation or suicide.

*

We commonly think that the only practical obstacle to writing poetry in Huizinga's sense is a lack of imaginative capacity, or material. If the only thing that I can imagine that the ATM 'represents' is a portal, or a door, and if the only thing that I can say about this door in *Get Rid of Yourself* is that an anarchist is trying to break it down, in order to 'get into' something impossible, a negative space that does not and cannot 'logically' exist, then the game that I am playing will quickly come to an end, like the three days of the 27th G8 Summit held in Genoa in 2001, or the two-day reign of Laigle, the 'neighbourhood dandy' in Emmanuel Le Roy Ladurie's *Carnival*:

> Laigle held his feasting for two days with all the gaiety and entertainments he could contrive so that during his reign, which lasted only the said two days, there was talk of nothing but masks, dances, the hunt, and other entertainments.[6]

After this, all comparisons are exhausted. Can we approach this differently? If the negative space on the 'other side' of the ATM is defined as the unexperienced or as yet uninvented, then the 'game' is defined in conventional terms: it ends once you run out of ideas. But if the negative space is defined as poetry 'as such', as the willingness and not the ability to say things that are untrue, then another, ulterior negative space opens up, entry to which is regulated not by our 'imaginative fertility' but by our willingness systematically to free ourselves from the many ties of obligation that inhibit us from so much as wanting to speak in this way, that is, in Huizinga's sense, poetically. Then we have two forms of negative space, or two negative capabilities superimposed on one another: the capacity to lie, but also the desire to do so.

The more ways in which (or even just *the more*) you feel able to smash the ATM to pieces, the larger is the area that this negative space defines. The point to keep in mind here is that this process is (contra Keats) an active one, meaning there are different ways to go about doing it. It is a practice, not a state. Because of this, it can be made into the subject of a game. The name of the game is getting rid of yourself.

For a long time now, poets have been in the habit of carrying out acts of perfect abstract negation upon themselves. They claim that society made them do it, and society counterclaims that they are being excessively sensitive. We are trained to think like this: to associate poetry with a special sensitivity or aversion to an abstraction, 'injustice'. But what about poetry as a special form of insensitivity? Can we imagine trying to *build* insensitivity? Can we imagine insensitivity workshops, insensitivity trainings, a poetics of insensitivity? There must be a sense in which this is what our reality already is; one, single, gigantic insensitivity bootcamp; in which case it would seem to follow that one task of poets is to understand that insensitivity and to exhibit it, and not merely to build fortified citadels of sensitivity all along its main roads and in its innermost peripheries.

One way to train ourselves to exhibit that insensitivity is to play games, including with perfect abstract negation itself. The perfect negation of how I myself 'feel' is one way into this poetry, by a simple act of denial; the *relationship* between this act and the poetics of metamorphosis, of changing physiognomies or outward appearances, is the substance of the 'poiesis' I am trying to describe. Inversion, negation and denial are simple means of this poeisis, but in order for them to remain so it is also necessary to be able to invert, negate and deny them. I admit that an aim of most of the poetry that I respect is to make it possible to find ways to survive, but I know that in doing so I am also saying more than I should, which is another way of saying speaking truthfully.

*

For now, let's stay with the ATMs.[7] The Automated Teller Machine, says Wikipedia, 'can be placed at any location but are most often ... near or inside banks, shopping centers/malls, airports, railway stations, metro stations, grocery stores, petrol/gas stations, restaurants, and other locations'.[8] It is dying: in 2019 in the UK 'an average of 340 machines disappear[ed] from high streets every month', smashed to pieces not predominantly by anarchist rioters but by the same social forces that earlier destroyed medieval feudal hierarchies, the poetic inversions of popular festivities, and kings, and which more recently has destroyed, or at least rendered painfully unfashionable, such more transient phenomena as the anti-globalisation movement, Situationist-inspired media activism, and the resonance of the once widespread belief that capitalism has provided the material basis for a universal and nearly permanent condition of carnivalesque abundance. 'ATMs are ... found on cruise ships and on some US Navy ships', says Wikipedia, 'where sailors can draw out their pay'. They 'may be on- and off-premises .... [and] ... in the US, Canada and some Gulf countries, banks may have drive-thru lanes providing access to ATMs using an automobile'. ATMs first appeared in their modern form in around 1973, approximately three million years after the appearance of the earliest hammers; 'poiesis' appeared sometime in between.

Everything I'm talking about here feels very dated. The blissful optout of smashing up an ATM already feels like an anachronistic symbol for an anarchist politics. Bernadette Corporation's film itself is a period piece. Getting a NY 'it girl'[9] (this language is itself now anachronistic) to read out the script of an insurrectionary anarchist like it's some kind of hilarious gag seems like a pretty tame criticism of 'the spectacle' when c. 2023 you pretty much can't *be* a celebrity until you've endorsed all of the latest radical-sounding demands, outsourcing any questions about how to implement them to a special class of eremites. How played out. How done.

> She spent like ten, fifteen minutes destroying the ATM screen.
> She looked crazy. She looked happy.
> It was a kind of joyful insanity.

I keep coming back to it though. The title of the film is itself a joke. It comes from a scene of the film in which Sevigny is unable to pronounce the word 'desubjectivisation'. She's reading from a passage of heavy Deleuzian jargon about 'capitalist schizophrenia', very serious philosophy voice, low pitch, very slow very deliberate, and then she fucks it up, De-Sub-Jec-Tiv-A-Tion, she laughs and the camera switches to show her lying on the floor face down next to a sofa, a kind of faceplant, and then it's back to the footage of police cars and the portentous monologue. Maybe it's a 'situationist' gag at her expense, maybe it's a 'situationist' gag at their own expense, I don't know; *the point is that it doesn't mean what it should.* The anarchist is smashing an ATM with a hammer, she is 'totally in her own world', she 'looked happy', 'It was a kind of joyful insanity', etc. Meanwhile, the ATM she is smashing to pieces *is no longer an ATM*, it doesn't represent itself, it 'represents' something more like Huizinga's logic and causality, we are watching it acquire a 'new physiognomy', a new face; but at the same time an inversion has taken place: subject and object have switched places, the anarchist now gets rid of *herself* by destroying the ATM, and for a limited period of time, for 'like ten, fifteen minutes', it is *herself* that she is attacking with a hammer, her own social physiognomy, and the reason why the insanity is joyful and not cruel or violent is that logic and causality do not apply here, there is no pain in this self-attack, it doesn't hurt.

(Violence should appear in poetry only to be separated from, or prevented from implying, pain. The ability to change every physiognomy is exactly that, an ability, with definite political and social uses. If what I am writing here appears to be a glib exercise in surrealism, it is because I want to talk about surrealism's immediate social and political uses, *as practice and technique.*)

Huizinga says, 'What the "others" do "outside" is no concern of ours at the moment. Inside the circle of the game the laws and customs of ordinary life no longer count. We are different and do things differently'.[10]

We are different, and we do things differently. 'Suppose', writes the musicologist Amiri Baraka, 'Negroes had been brought to this country to make vases or play basketball.

How might the blues have developed then from the impetus of work songs geared to those occupations'?[11] Suppose they had been brought (t)here to make hammers, or ATMs: 'I saw her all by herself, smashing up an ATM machine with a hammer ... Thrashing at the ATM machine. Hammering away.'

> She looked crazy. She looked happy. It was a kind of joyful insanity.

To get into the circle Huizinga describes, the 'space' of poetics, you've got to first leave the 'outside' behind. This entails a movement through a threshold-state.[12] Entering this state, you may feel a painful sense of attachment to those meanings that you have resolved to leave behind. This feeling enters into conflict with the desire that you now act upon, which, within the context of those meanings, is always something really stupid, really distortive and ignorant and totally contrary to all of your own 'beliefs', 'convictions' etc. In *Get Rid of Yourself*, this threshold-state comes up explicitly, slightly earlier in the dialogue in which the smashing of the ATM is described, when Sevigny, reading the words of an anarchist, says

> In the middle of the first day the whole thing happened, I ran into an old friend of mine I hadn't seen in months.
> I saw her all by herself, smashing up an ATM machine with a hammer.
> She seemed completely in her own world.
> A year ago, we had a little argument about street violence.

She was hesitating, really resisting the idea.

If I stand between the space I think of as 'literary criticism', and another space in which I feel I can enter only if I entertain my desire to say or do something really dumb, something really deeply dumb and untrue both of 'my own convictions' and of the poems that I strip-mine for metaphors and images, but whose sense I couldn't really give a fuck about, I find myself hesitating, 'really resisting the idea'. I have a kind of hammer in my hand, and I seem to be in some kind of vase factory. It radiates out from under me in a kind of painfully inflated circle, a glass cockpit in negative space.

In her book *Social History of the Fool*, Sandra Billington talks about the theological origins of the idiot in the following terms:

> As western Europe became Christianised "fool" initially retained St Paul's meaning and meant the witless man. The two early English court jesters were not known by anything other than *joculator* and minstrel. The closeness of the witless man to God was stressed, since the innocent of the natural has links with Christian or Pauline folly ... whereas the church continued its protection of the witless man, an awareness developed of the need to distinguish such men from their mimics who were beginning to profit from the idiot's immunity from work in the houses of the great.[13]

The desire to say or do something 'witless' is related, paradoxically but by a deep roping vein of historical experience, to the desire to be innocent. In behaving like an 'artificial fool', I *demand* the treatment that is accorded to the 'innocent', i.e., to that person who according to the Church is not and cannot be held responsible for their actions, and who, furthermore (at least in the thinking of some early Christian theologians) is a sign or symbol on this earth of the divine.[14] That is to say, *because* I am smashing an automated teller machine to pieces with a hammer, I declare myself innocent. A censored version of this most basic gesture of centuries of popular 'play' was belatedly introduced to the mainstream of literary history by the poet Friedrich Schiller, who says, in his 'On Naïve and Sentimental Poetry', that the poet is 'constituted' by the fact that 'he annuls everything in himself that recalls an artificial world'.[15] Witlessness for Schiller is a pure negative: everything in himself [sic] that recalls an artificial world', all knowledge, is annulled. By this means innocence is purified of its origins in popular class rule-breaking (legitimised and sustained as 'play'), severed from the joyful ceremonial stupidity of the false king, rhetorically deloused, and prescribed for poets of delicate sensibilities or sensitivities as a kind of purge.

Is there a sense in which the Schillerian idea of the purge acts as a substitute for a popular poetics, with its tradition of social inversion, fooling or witlessness, and negative capability? And is it possible that this substitution inaugurates another transition, from poetics as a means of practical self-defence (of culpability refused) to poetics as a means of individualised self-harm, in the form of purgation or auto-annulment? In any case, everywhere I look I encounter instances of the Schillerian attitude. A recent version in the world of contemporary poetry is a poem by Ariana Reines, 'Sandra Bland', titled after the black lawyer who in 2015 was randomly abducted into the US prison system and found dead in her prison cell several days later. Reines concludes her poem,

> I'd like to do a language purge & see
>
> If God grant me the peace enough to see it thru
>
> I'd like to see
>
> When it's over if it ever ends if there's anything left
>
> Of the power in frailty (etc.)[16]

Here, the wish to be innocent dovetails with the desire to eject things from your mind, to annul them, to rip or bleed them out. In this lyrical adaptation of the 'Classical' Aristotelian idea of an emotional purge or *katharsis*, with its roots in an earlier medical tradition of abjection or menstruation, the relationship between witlessness as irresponsibility, and naivety as 'childlike innocence' etc., gets lost. As a result, the poetic significance of the popular and festive desire for irresponsibility likewise disappears. Innocence/naivety/stupidity etc. is a zero, a nothing, a blank, a pure α that remains after lyric poets have blasted 'language' out of their own heads like player-characters in some firstperson shooter. It is 10.35 a.m. α too disintegrates into a smear of anger and revulsion, like the exploding heads in David Cronenberg's *Scanners*. Tomorrow this will perhaps happen again, and if I can't do it then someone else will, and by this means a certain tradition of poetry is perpetuated. 'We erase ourselves through self hatred', writes June Jordan.[17] I like this poem by Ariana Reines: unlike 99% of work written right now, or I suppose ever, it cares enough about poetry to set it some practical tasks and then tries to play them out, through and within the physical realities of our decaying and awkward bodies. But I don't think it has much to say about how to get into the circle I've been talking about, or what it's like for the like ten, fifteen minutes we get to stay there, and I am sick of people I care for shooting themselves metaphorically in the head.

We are different, and we do things differently.

*

It may now be worth running through last week's episode: Bernadette Corporation's 2003 film *Get Rid of Yourself* contains a theory of poetry. The theory has some resemblance to Situationist arguments about play, as well as to the anthropological accounts of initiation rites from which those arguments were derived. The theory says we exist at the edge of a circle. For so long as we exist on this edge, we are obliged to mean what we say. Truth imposes itself on us and in my own role as (say) a literary critic I should say what I 'think' about such things as films and poems as well as the historical realities into and against which they scrape their way, painfully. It is not acceptable to lie. All around the circumference of this circle small ramparts appear; they are made of what the Chloë Sevigny character calls 'little arguments': we can have them with ourselves, or with our friends. You say you 'ought' to go inside: this argument paradoxically forms a part of the ramparts, it isn't the same as going there. 'Poetry, what's it for | Comes from "doing" | Means "Do It"', writes Sean Bonney, channelling Katerina Gogou.[18] 'Read no more / see! / see no more / go!', writes Paul Celan.[19] 'She was hesitating, really resisting the idea', says Chloë Sevigny, both before and later.

Again and again, the only way into and through that circle is a piece of mass produced electronic equipment. 'The theft of large refrigerators by people with no electricity', write the Situationists, 'is the best image of the lie of affluence transformed into a truth by play'.[20] 'I couldn't avoid the word | dashcam and I wouldn't | Even try but for some reason something within me is angry | Also at the ugliness of that word', writes Raines. 'I saw her all by herself, smashing up an ATM machine with a hammer ...', reads Sevigny. 'Thrashing at the ATM machine. Hammering away.'

The dashcam, the large refrigerator and especially the ATM or cash machine are the border guards at the edge of this circle that we want to get into but are constantly turned away from by our own clever desire to say the truth as we feel and perceive it, and which again and again drives us to write versions of an essay that across all of its tedious drafts and fragments says nothing except the same thing, that we are bored and alone and feel a perfectly objective despair. They, these square machines with their own distinctive insides and outsides, are sphinxes, also relics or runes in the sense of the art historian Andre Jollés, in that they constitute themselves as 'objects charged with the power of a form which, in their concreteness, incarnate the form as a whole'.²¹ In the riddle of the sphinx, Jollés continues, 'The riddler may not confront the guesser in the terrible form of a monster who threatens to throttle him, but we still sense the compulsion: the access to that conceded thing is a matter of life and death, both for the one demanding entry and for the one granting it'.²² 'It is the guesser's achievement to break through to something that has been sealed off'.²³ It is so obvious and so easy to see the anarchist's friend here, smashing ... with a hammer ... Thrashing .... Hammering away.

> She looked crazy. She looked happy. It was a kind of joyful insanity.

The sphinx is the ATM, its screen is the riddle, the cash it 'conceals' its first and most obvious solution. At the same time, the word at the centre of Reines' line approaches the limit case for 'artificiality' as Schiller first described it. 'Camera' is a Latin term meaning 'arch' and latterly a piece of Western twentieth-century visual technology, now associated with a rectangle we carry around with us and misleadingly refer to as a phone; dashboard is a compound construction which continues to be used to describe the interior driver display of mass produced automobiles, even though these are no longer made of 'board' and, not facing outward, a fortiori cannot have dirt or mud thrown or 'dashed' against them. 'Dashcam' is a compound built out of these compounds and a further alienation from the source of desire, a word which carries its meaninglessness and inappositeness in its bowels like a tumour everyone can sense even though they cannot see it. We live like this, dashcam, ash can, trashcam and cash machine, ashes on a street in the world of legend, in the world of myth, that is to say in this world, ours, with its many layers of ramifying spitefulness and silence. In Genoa in 2001 or London in 2011 or Minneapolis in 2021. Marx also talked about riddles and sphinxes, first explicitly in his early writings when he argued that 'Communism is the riddle of history solved',[24] and then more obliquely in his later 'mature' Preface. Fuck that stupid worn-out phrase. Jollés: 'Every actualization contains within itself not only the possibility of a solution, but also the solution itself'.[25]

In the enemy language it is necessary to lie. The cash machine, the cassa or box, this square, this black box that we are always hearing about and which is supposed to mean indeterminacy or possibility or chance, though in reality all of these things are governed algorithmically and according to the system logic of probability, this square exists at the centre of a circle. This square is a sphinx, a riddle with two solutions. Jolles: 'The riddler who encrypts also betrays himself in his own riddle. Here a new riddle inserts itself into the riddle ... There are riddles that have a harmless solution in female company, a less harmless one in male company'.[26] The first solution to the destruction of that square is simply that it is a metaphor, a bad one, she (the friend of the anarchist) is smashing to pieces the cash machine because it 'represents' money, the money system, etc: it is an instance of synecdoche. He (the Watts rioter) has stolen the large refrigerator though he cannot use it because he is superior to commodities (and the Situationists had never heard of the second-hand market): it is a metonym. This is the solution to the riddle of the destruction of the ATM that is available to us at the edge of the circle. It is the one that Bernadette Corporation disclose to their own 'female company', the famous 90s actor Chloë Sevigny, reproducing for a new audience the misogynistic intelligence that is described (and presumably approved of) by the Nazi André Jolles.[27] But there is a second solution that inserts itself into this riddle. We are inside the circle because the square no longer means anything to us, the access to that concealed thing, the cash in the cash machine, the food in the large refrigerator, the footage in the dashcam, is no longer a matter of life and death, the sphinx has disappeared along with our sense of responsibility to an audience and for like ten or fifteen minutes all that we are doing is playing, like children, in a game whose rules we are not able, and that we do not want, to describe. You may make clever ironic films about the spectacularisation of radical theory, you may write earnest poems about wanting to set police cars on fire, you may write resentful essays about how jejune this is and how played out: What the 'others' do 'outside' is no concern of ours at the moment. We are different, and we do things differently.

*

Heinrich Heine once wrote a book at the end of which he described a dream:

> *Last night I dreamt of a large desert forest and a glum autumn night. In the large desolate forest, between the sky-high trees, light places appeared from time to time, but they were filled with a ghostly white fog. Here and there from the thick fog issued a quiet forest fire. Walking towards one of them, I*

noticed all sorts of dark shadows moving around the flames; but it was only in the immediate vicinity that I could make out the slender figures and their melancholy, fair faces. They were beautiful, naked female images, like the nymphs we see in the lascivious paintings of Julio Romano, gracefully reclining in luxuriant youthful blossom under a canopy of deciduous foliage and lusting ... Alas! no such cheerful spectacle presented itself here to my sight! The women of my dream, although still adorned with the charm of eternal youth, nevertheless bore a secret destruction in body and being; The limbs were still enchanting with sweet symmetry, but somewhat emaciated and as if overchilled with cold misery, and even in the faces, despite the smiling lightness, the traces of an abysmal grief were twitching. Also, instead of on swelling lawn benches, like the nymphs of Julio, they crouched on the hard ground under half-defoliated oak trees, where, instead of the amorous sunlight, the whirling vapors of the damp autumn night sintered down upon them ... Sometimes one of these beauties would rise, seize a blazing fire from the brushwood, swing it over her head like a thyrsus, and attempt one of those impossible dance poses we've seen on Etruscan vases ... but smiling sadly, as if overcome by fatigue and night cold, she sank back to the crackling fire. One in particular among these women moved my whole heart with an almost voluptuous pity. I don't know how it happened, but before I knew it I was sitting beside her by the fire, busy warming her frost-shivering hands and feet to my burning lips; also playing with her black damp tresses of hair that hung down over the Greek straight-nosed face and the touchingly cold, barren bosom . . . .

While she now lay on my knees and slumbered, sometimes gasping like a dying woman in her sleep, her companions whispered all sorts of conversations, of which I understood very little, since they pronounced Greek quite differently from that I had learned at school, and later also from old Wolf... . . . Only so much I understood, that they complained about the bad time and still feared a worsening of the same, and intended to flee still deeper into the forest Then suddenly, in the distance, there rose a clamor of raw mob voices ... They shouted, I don't remember what: (a shouting of raw voices) "Long live the Republic!" [later improved to: "Long live Lamennais!"). - The editor]. . . . In between, a Catholic bell giggled ... And my beautiful forest women became visibly even paler and leaner, until they finally melted completely into mist, and I myself awoke yawning.[28]

I first read this book about a decade ago. The image of emaciated nymphs fleeing ever further into a deserted forest has always stayed with me. In my imagination, this forest is a perfect circle. Heine's nymphs are always running towards a non-existent centre: 'Time and lighting are unrecognizable: [they] are "fleeing towards paradise"; and "all clocks and calendars" are ... to be "broken" or, rather, "forbidden"'.[29] At the non-existent centre of this forest is a square, a dashcam, a large refrigerator, a cash machine, a four-sided negative space of nonexistence or contradiction towards which all mythological figures flee. But there is always a further depth of the forest to flee into, the chase never ends, and so neither does the process of the nymphs' decomposition, and in the end they are so emaciated they look like anarchists carrying hammers in Genoa in 2001, and we look on like Chloë Sevigny in *Get Rid of Yourself* as our comrade moves towards the centre of this circle that does not exist and into the negative inner space of a cash machine (or a forest) which only comes to be because we are running into it, hammering away with a crude tool of perfect abstract negation. So that for like ten, fifteen minutes this feels like all there is: to enter the circle in which poetry is possible is the only poetry we need. The 'nymphs' looked crazy. They looked happy.

It was a kind of joyful insanity.

It may be true that we are running away from ourselves. It may be a lie to say that this game of perfect abstract negation is the only poetry we need; but then running away is the alternative to becoming the victims of a self-organised mental pogrom. The *raw mob voices* that in Heine's dream at first call out the slogans of the republic and then the slogans of the king take us to the edge of the circle where we began, with the popular games of the festival or the world turned upside down, the voices of the Stalinists and homophobes who have fucked up my head for years and who think they are still playing, though they have not realised that inversion is an important kind of play only for like ten, fifteen minutes, that its significance is that it is an easy way to play, not that it is intrinsically a way to overcome hierarchy, and that it is easiness that we need to learn to create for ourselves, for our class, and not self-consuming ressentiment and its many accompanying forms of boredom and inverted mental death.

and I myself awoke yawning

Letter to Dom Hale

so we travel together under an intense wind
sweat on our backs, our mouths dry

a poem not for 'the universe', but right here
among houses & scorned trees
in the arms of other people

towards what refuses demolition

        Dom Hale

Dear Dom,

How are you? Since I last wrote I've had time to read *Ill Pips* at last and to read through SEIZURES again and again, as well as Tom Crompton's DEFINITIONS.[30] I've been back in the UK since September, experiencing the same objective conditions as everybody. Also I've started to feel this new itch of what I think might be (but it's hard to say, it's been so long since it's been like this) – the only word I know for it is *clarity*, a kind of sudden onset of lucidity about what I need to think and to say and do, and the books you've put out have been an essential part of that sense, for me, and I want to say here something about what it seems to me like your book in particular is doing, or at least how it makes me feel: the swirl or smear of references that it paints across the surface of my mind.

Perhaps another name for clarity is disillusionment. Recently I've *felt* that I have been disillusioned, but for me that state of being doesn't fall out the way that I would have expected it to. I mean that I always thought disillusionment would be identical to vengeful disappointment and ressentiment, but in fact the kind of ideological nakedness that I feel right now isn't like that at all, and I look around me and see everywhere new work that is similarly disillusioned and sees clearly what it is possible to do. I'll say at the end of this text a little bit more about what I think your poem has to say about this state, about the death of old myths. I think it has to do with scorn, and about justifying ourselves. And none of this is straightforward; the earlier poets who've helped me to think about this the most usually committed suicide or medicated themselves to death: no one is writing self-help books in verse; it's not even about happiness exactly, it's about knowing what to do and who for, and I think that there is a feeling and a tone that is associated with that knowing and that that's what you've described to me and what I want now to try to speak back to you, if I can.

*

And I've been thinking about the idea of 'defence' again. Your book (and Tom's DEFINITIONS, which is its twin) seems to have a kind of intellectual relation to that idea, in the sense that both works are committed to thinking through what the principles of community self-defence and mutual aid as represented by the Poets' Hardship Fund might look like *in poetry*.[31] Their 'public purpose' comes back in here as an effort at self-clarification in this one specific sense, as a shared effort to seize some aesthetic space and to begin the work of defining it. (I also think this doesn't contradict the statement in the Intro to *Ill Pips*, that 'the solidarities you'll find by doing these things are far richer than any aesthetic affinities, cliques or other shit that you pretend to care about'.[32] The point here is to think through the politics from the poetry, not the other way round. Also, you're both writing poems, not instructions for poems. I am sorry for writing something so obvious.)

So SEIZURES seems to me like a very beautiful defence, perfect in its openness and lyrical disfigurement, and the most beautiful thing about it for me is its passionate claim to a kind of collective being. This poetry, yours, is *ours*, it says. It is us, it is 'our music', to borrow a phrase from Ornette Coleman that it would be crass to introduce here if it wasn't so obviously true: since it is. The book is programmatic like this: it knows this about itself and proposes for us an organising metaphor. If poetry is a 'small patch of ground' (5), a divot, a scrap or patch of turf or black sod dislodged by a horse's hoof or (better) by the swing of some fucker's golf club, then still this has no bearing on its meaning to us, since we fight for it knowing it is the only thing that we possess; and because our ability to articulate a 'we' IS the only thing worth defending. 'The ardent desire for an "us" to survive the horror and the annihilation' (as Elsa Dorling puts it in her book *Self Defense*) is capable of being realised on or within this 'small patch' of shared language by means of the struggle for it; and this is why we will do anything to hold on to it, and this is why we need to feel it being torn from us, and why the question of its size seems so ludicrously misplaced.[33]

It's a beautiful book, and unless I try to get this down quickly I know that my own pessimism will prevent me from describing it rightly. The passage of a few people through a brief period of time is easy to narrate in a tone of bankrupt nostalgia. It is much harder to transmit into language in the process of its becoming, with the consciousness of its fragility clear and present and yet still undistorted into its successor-states of fatalism or cynicism or defeatism. Büchner: 'I have been studying the history of the French Revolution. I have felt as if crushed beneath the gruesome fatalism of History ... The individual mere froth on the wave, greatness sheer chance ... a ridiculous struggle against brazen law'.[34] 'I will never not stand by you' (9). The double negatives are the essentially lyrical element of this promise, and of all the other promises that the book makes besides, which is to say the truth of them as a kind of tissue of falsehoods and provisionalities that we use to climb up towards one another, in the knowledge that anything sturdier would snap in our hands above abysses of whatever happens to be in the news.

I'll try to put that less rhapsodically. One thing the PHF has done for our 'scene' is introduce into it a tacit polemic for politics as something that we do, not something we distantly contemplate. That change of perspective has initiated some belated recognitions. For one thing, it's held up a kind of mirror in which some of us start to see that WE ARE IN the environment that we observed.

> Lies nicht mehr – schau!
> Schau nicht mehr – geh!

And I think this begins to show up the difficulties that we're faced with. It has to do with the negatives. I will never not. I will not, I never, I can't. We've got to be able to say what we *can't* do as well as what we can. I know this in the same way I know the haze in my head and the tightness around my eyes. And the issue isn't just about being able to say 'no', as in the history of political refusal brilliantly orchestrated in (for example) the essays of Anne Boyer.[35] Or rather, it is but it isn't: it's about the ability to say no to our own friends and comrades as well, the feeling that in order to be and to act freely we have to be able to behave in ways that seem ugly and irresponsive, and that poetry will always be a lie unless we can find ways to communicate this at the same time as we say with conviction that we will make our own culture and that we will be enough for one another and that we believe this, that it is a kind of destiny to say fuck their platforms and their promotion drives and their tiny little ersatz passions that make a mockery of what we need, and feel.

So you need to be able to cultivate a certain kind of defencelessness and naivety in relation to the limits of what we can presently do. This is incidentally, I mean essentially, why I love the late poetry of Jack Spicer: because when I read him I feel so irrefutably the mind of someone who is still a child, and with a child's weakness and a child's imprescriptible demand to be loved, and a child's irresponsibility, even though they are, though Spicer clearly was, an adult human male, a large decaying mind suddenly dropped at the end of its life like a hostage dumped in a field. With the lights of its earlier self still twinkling out on the horizon. And because I've been watching an unusual amount of TV lately I can say that the figure of Little Brother in the early Lars von Trier TV show *The Kingdom* is a fantastically Spicer-esque figure, the most Spicer-esque there is, a beautiful soul ripped to pieces by the enormity of its own body and (tacitly) by the things we have been driven to do to it. 'This / is the opposite of a party or a social gathering'.[36] Clearly. 'The / Bumble-bee there cruising over a few poor flowers'.[37] 'I confess myself, like them, unwilling to be stunned by the Theseids of the hoarse Codri of the day'.[38] The ground still not fixed as I / thought it would be in an adult world.[39] Famously, Spicer's late book *Language* has its title scrawled over an issue of the academic journal *Language*, in which is contained an article about linguistics co-written by the younger, stronger Jack Spicer. More and more this feels to me like the only historical-poetic manifesto I can sort of get behind. *First* learn to write down your ideas, *then* learn again how to write all of your lurid political and intellectual and intimate disappointments and all of your childhood hopes over the top of them, so that both are still visible, impossible, infuriating and banal in their patterns of mutual interference. I think this *is* what poetry feels like for me, when it happens. Only language scratched on walls exists, the tags and illegal marks and scribbles of a speech that is trying to impress itself on, to push itself into, or to leave the tracks of its fingernails across the face of some kind of hostile environment, uh huh, uh huh, poetry as 'organized violence committed on ordinary speech', that remark by Roman Jakobson from *On Czech Poetry* that everyone assumes is about 'literature' in general.[40]

So Spicer's poetry as the revolting body of the adult child, which with its broken helpless limbs of quotation and mishearing speaks beautifully in a language of hope and agonising incomprehension. This is our music. 'Institutions have not only shaped our demands but also in the most literal sense our logic, or sense of proportion'.[41] And when you write 'I need you to take my lines towards the others' (3), the situation I imagine is exactly this one, the situation where helpless dependency and mutilation and the ability to speak sweetly and (and this is so important) uncomprehendingly are all bound up together and can only be separated by a kind of fucking fascist cruelty that we persist in calling thinking, and writing. Yola. Your line here is filled with pronouns that are hard to pin down: the 'you' and 'the others' themselves shadowy, indistinct: the adverb 'towards' (which recurs again – jarringly, I think – in the book's final line) itself a marker of incompletion. So that the lines will never reach their destination but will only 'counter-journey' towards them like teams of polar explorers (7), or Romantic deserters from some insane lexical army ('defeatists who deserted their poems' (9))... but with the faint invocation here also of the relay race, or of that now very famous dictum of di Prima's: 'get started, | someone will finish'.[42] (But di Prima's 'someone', her 'someone else', is a deus ex machina, a ghost in the machine of revolt: and your emphasis is on the need that burns through that political faith and cries out for a 'you' / a 'someone else' who is real and alive and here and not a figment of political convictions which have become unbearable to us because their grammar is auxiliary and indirect and our needs are really pretty immediate now, to the point we don't even know anymore what we'll do if we can't meet them. Spicer's helpless demand, di Prima's beautiful imperative. Suicide, and its auxiliary form of grace. I think we probably get to choose whether or not to have this thought: but not its mood, which in turn is what really determines the kind of poetry we write.

One more note and then I'll try to finish with these preliminaries. Tags and scribbles and scratch marks are too easy to read as metaphors for the kind of language that interests me; the idea then would be that poetic language should be 'like' a medium applied to a surface, should be 'like' an act of criminal damage etc. This is the enforcement of a conventional hierarchy of genres:

graffiti is a lower form of art (a 'lesser art') and poetry takes inspiration from it by turning it into a source of metaphors for its own privileged activity: my knowledge and beliefs are 'like' a wall, the poems that I write are 'like' an act of calculated vandalism that I perform upon their surface. All of those adverbs of comparison are a means of mystification. Actually, it is the real social practice of writing on walls that created the possibility for this kind of poetry, it *is* the poetry, if we still want to call it that, and poets who come to think of their poetry as a way of vandalising the thoughts in their own head just copy it – are 'literally' engaged in copying, in other words; metaphor doesn't come in to it. And this is not the only kind of demotion that I think we need to accept if we want to think about how to keep writing poetry. (Less significantly, also, it implies a departure from Spicer's definition of poetry; Spicer was insistent that bad poems consist of the things you 'want' to say, whereas I am convinced that I do *want* to write badly and clumsily all over the surface of my own thoughts and feelings, with a hammer if necessary, with a laptop or a notebook if I can.)[43]

Maybe I can say something now about the final poem in the book:

> so we travel together under an intense wind
> sweat on our backs, our mouths dry
>
> a poem not for 'the universe', but right here
> among houses & scorned trees
> in the arms of other people

    towards what refuses demolition (11)

Here it seems to me that the earlier line is corrected in some sense. The Spicerian demand (I need other people, I am helpless, I will destroy myself and everything I touch if you don't hear me) becomes something much more affirmative; but it is still different from the di Primaesque imperative. The 'other people' are *known* now, they are neither agonisingly distant ('the others' I need you to take my lines towards) and nor are they the mere notion of comrades as the mirrors of those gigantic shadows which futurity casts upon the present. They are right here; and we are in their arms and in the same towns where they live the idea takes hold of us that it is these self-destructive Spicerian people, with their meannesses and their dependencies, who are the only universe we need...

And I've thought a lot about those 'scorned trees'. I went away for a week and stopped writing this and now I'm back and they're still here, standing very still, very black and cold in my head. Scorn related to *skern*, to mockery or jest; since we *laugh to scorn* those who strike us as pathetic or absurd. Scorned as in a lower art form, like the graffiti on the wall, or Pierre Bourdieu's family photography, or the poetry that 'everyone' writes when they suffer a personal loss, or the circus and its rigid hierarchy of clowns. Etc.[44]

It has taken me a long time to be among them. For a long time I thought I had an obligation to my comrades who it seemed to me were more hurt than I was, and I even wrote a poem about this once that finished with those words, one of the few I have written that I thought was any good after I had written it, and it was only much later on that I began to feel about this sense of obligation that it was itself a kind of mutilation, a way of being that had found its way into me from some much deeper recess of personal or 'generational' history, that I was damaged by that obligation and that it was preventing me from feeling anything for myself, that I was like one of Hölderlin's stupid gods who only feel vicariously and need humans to suffer on their behalf,[45] and that this mutilation meant that for me, like Büechner's monkey, there was something essentially grotesque about my expressive personhood, a naivety that was not beautiful because 'untaught' and 'spontaneous' but ugly because clumsy and lowclass. Contemptible. To be scorned.

And here's another end-of-year thought. My favourite album of 2022 came out in 2020, it's called *Another Country*.[46] I feel this is the most poetic gesture imaginable. Fuck another world, the bloated and superfluous idea of an equivalent to the thing that we feel compelled to renounce: if we needed that kind of insurance policy, where would the violence and the hatred for this reality be? The trees sway a little in the wind and seem to ask us this: if we make another country with our work (I don't just mean 'with our poetry'), and if it was SCORN that animated its composition, the scorn that they pour on us, *would this new country of our invention be made of scorn*, right down to the level of its sky and its clouds and its earth and its ugly residential trees? Would those scorned trees look the same as the huge green nameless tree / breathing pretty quiet overhead?[47] I ask because I think your poetry might be capable of telling me, I mean it seriously as a question.

I know this is too diffuse, that I am trying to say too many things at once. I sometimes think that poetry might be a kind of *training* in how to want things without justification (whether moral or simply rational, as in, *I want this* without any guarantee that it is possible to have). I understand that with this thought I simply displace to a higher level an even more basic desire, for poetry to have a stable and communicable purpose, which when I am depressed or doubtful manifests itself as the impatient desire for poems to solve all my problems or tell me what the world means. Fanny Howe: 'I think my problem from childhood has been my longing for a system to explain the world ... It would have been better to study human behaviour and foibles. Instead, I wanted to know what everything meant. In one word'.[48] Like Howe, I know this, but I commit to this childish and needy displacement because I recognise that whether or not poetry can do this for me, I *need* this training and my ability to speak and think in ways that I value is destined to wither and spark out in its absence. In other words I need to be able to want things that I am myself likely to think about or treat with scorn. I want to live in another country. I want to write poems in which that desire expresses itself with the kind of deadout problematic sentimentality that you find in the love poems of a dying alcoholic who is drinking himself to death in the year 1964 and in whose beautiful hopes and impossible desires are twisted and malformed all the nerves of his body that is visibly collapsing and breaking down, into poems scarred by solecism and the simplest errors of judgment and the most desperate repetitions. I want to live in ANOTHER COUNTRY and I want to want this more than the intelligence that tells me that this is the wrong thing to want (too simple, too theoretically crude, too redolent of a 'dangerous' nationalism blah blah blah.) It is difficult for me to write 'about' poetry (as I am doing now) without going through several tedious attempts to tie up all the loose ends, it's a tic of my education, I learned it too early to ever get rid of it completely, but at least the way in which I'm doing it now is in the service of the way of life in which I and you and all of us no longer give a shit about what they think. I recognise in this a small kind of advance, and I accept it for what it is –

with the madman's complicitous love of his illness.[49]

Scorn is related to laughter both etymologically and lexically. We laugh our enemies to scorn and in doing so we recall the Germanic roots of a word that means both cutting and joking, jesting and tearing open. Scorn which is *dripped* on us reminds us that laughter bursts out from above and is directed at what is below, at what is 'infinitely vile and base' and howling in the pangs of its poison (Baudelaire).[50] It occurs to me that there are fewer jokes in the contemporary poetry that I value than there were in the poetry that I grew up with, and when I think positively about this it is because I think we no longer feel ourselves to be superior to anything at all:

> Birds and animals – not all, but many of them – understand the language of plants. Plants understand the language of stones. Stones understand the language of dots. (Evgenia

Belorusets)[51]

I think that poetry should train us to understand the language of dots. That would mean wanting things that induce scorn or contempt, which means not only things that educated people think are 'impossible' (the usual abstractions) but also things which most people *don't need to want* because they can simply fucking have them. Most people in this shitty country still don't *need* to want food, though several million people do, and they are the only ones whose opinion matters both from the perspective of poetry and also of whatever it is that 'politics' is. Probably the most contemptible idea for existing 'society' (including for a lot of academic leftism) is the idea that you just want to hold on to what you have, nation state or city street or home or room or lover or child or consciousness of the feeling of sweat on our backs, our mouths dry. Everything that merely exists, that's not able to fucking justify itself. Even if it's worth nothing, is a refugee camp or slum or a street market filled with fish-heads and plastic awnings:

> Typical of the trees found in myth is the tree of paradise, or tree of life; most people know of the pine-tree of Attis, the tree of trees of Mithras, and the world-ash Yggdrasill of Nordic mythology, and so on. The hanging of Attis, in effigy, on a pine-tree, the hanging of Marsyas, which became a popular theme for art, the hanging of Odin, the Germanic hanging sacrifices and the whole series of hanged gods – all teach us that the hanging of Christ on the cross is nothing unique in religious mythology, but belongs to the same circle of ideas.

> In this world of images the Cross is the Tree of Life
> and at the same time a Tree of Death – a coffin.[52]

So one more time with feeling: I've thought a lot about the 'scorned trees'. The most scorned or contemptible idea of all is the idea you just want to hold on to what you have, *for no other reason than that you have it,* because it is present in our lives and we experience it and not at the mythical centre of the universe or at the root of a new world but *here* and *now* in our arms which in their own circle form a magic defence against all the people who know what they want and how to get it. I see the trees at the end of SEIZURES as an antithesis to that world-tree, this tree of trees with its perfect geometry of meaning, but this doesn't mean it has anything to do with 'realism'; it is a little shoplift song, an attempt to steal the light of that mythical reality and carry it back out into the everyday, the ordinary and the diurnal. You said to me after I sent you the first draft of this that you wanted to write poems that take care of people, and yourself, and I have also been trying to think through what that means, in a culture that always tells you in your face and coercively to do exactly that. It's obvious to me that wanting poetry to 'train' us to do or want anything means to speak from, and in some sense to affirm, a position of serious weakness, the functional language of a society that says you should know what everything is for and be able to take care of yourself, but I have also come to reject the obvious alternatives. June Jordan wrote that we erase ourselves with self hatred. Paul Celan threw himself into the river Seine on 20 April 1970. Büchner died of typhus aged 23. My birthday is April 19th. We erase ourselves as poets in that we annul everything in us that recalls an artificial world (Schiller). Hart Crane threw himself off some kind of ridiculous boat. Georges Jacque Danton died on the 5th of April, 1794. Fabre, who in Büchner's *Danton's Death* says he would like to die 'twice', was guillotined on the same day, once. June Jordan was still alive in 2002. She wrote about her love for Walt Whitman, who said that I exist as I am, that is enough.[53]

And we are right here. As we start to think about politics as something we 'do', and no longer as a History we are crushed beneath, despair ceases to be (as J.H. Prynne once put it) a model question.[54] We return into ourselves, and as we learn to fucking value ourselves again, the intensity with which we experience even the small patch of ground on which we act becomes greater than the intensity of grief we felt for the large one on which we blatantly didn't. Also we come to feel that we cannot respond to the imperatives of our friends unless we're able to articulate some demands of our own, and the undecideability of the relationship of demand and imperative in our lives becomes one of the motives to write shit like this, which is the red crayon or stub of lipstick we use to remind ourselves of who we are, across the covers of all the journals and newspapers and superegoic slogans that tell us to forget it. 'Start from your yard', is what it says in *Ill Pips*. Once again these traces (lipstick traces) of di Prima.

And like I said your book is beautiful because it is a very naked statement of this desire to have a life outside of that forgetting-system, the enormous temperature-controlled space of a middle-class culture that suffocates everything it contains and undermines everything it asserts: that is content to speak from inside of the thing that it pretends decorously to reject. It thematises that desire and makes a fucking polemic on its behalf, names the moment and puts its head above the parapet. I know that by talking in this way about 'taking care of one another' with our poems, or 'training' ourselves to think in different ways, we lessen ourselves. That we make what we know will be perceived as a lesser art. That we become less than what we were. That we have a sense of how ridiculous we are. In trying to find some meaning in the most abject vocabulary of individualised crisis management, we are contaminated by the sources of that vocabulary in a way that is hard to come back from. Finally we accept that contamination. In a similar vein I admire an essay by Sarah Brouillette, on the novels of Sally Rooney, in which she points out the disavowed and moralised relationship between Rooney's representation of sex 'scenes' and what literary figures and gatekeepers might want to parenthesise or frame as actual sex work.[55] There is nothing noble about what we are doing. But we have trained ourselves to do it.

So whatever. Dear Dom, I want to know what the costs are of committing ourselves to our patch of ground like this. I've talked about the Spicerian body as this enormous horrific dying thing, I suppose maybe because I feel that way about myself too, because I feel this incredible painful naivety in me, and then I read an obituary for a person I met in passing a couple of times over the last ten years and I shudder because it says something I don't want to be true. 'I know', says the obituary writer, that in the end she (the deceased) knew 'that neither god, nor communism, nor "each other" was sufficient'.⁵⁶ I tried to argue with the last part of that statement but I can't, I can only feel nearer or closer to it, which is what this naivety I'm talking about is, a kind of terrible beautiful defencelessness which is also weightlessness, and exposure to the change of the wind.

> the sun will rise so that men come out of women again
> translucent so you can see their silver
> circulatory systems and
> bullets flow through them and get tangled in the nets
> of veins … as in their hearts

which is Galina Rymbu, writing her own naïve and sentimental poetry, copied off Facebook and then Englished in Google Translate so I can see roughly what it means. And she is writing about Another Country as well. The people we know are dysfunctional with well-developed instincts towards flight. We need to be able to promise to one another a language in which it is possible to be sincere. The poetry I care about knows this and sheds its myths, its illusions. It drifts across its own beliefs and convictions like they were landscapes across which it is blown. Defencelessly. And because of this it is alive, and translucent. I think your book is translucent. And like I said before: clarity is what we need now, it gives me more strength than anything.

Much love,
Danny

Five Reports[57]
(i) 'early march, illegal migration bill'
14 March 2023

so it's a sunday night and i'm at a poetry reading in london. the floor is sticky with beer and i can feel its residue on the backs of my jeans. i'm here on my own even though i'm surrounded by people who i've known for as long as I've been reading poetry: 'twenty years older, with the skulls plainer in their faces', as per the one line that sticks with me from orwell's book about the second world war (the one about unicorns and shopkeepers). one of them's on stage now; he's asking himself what it would be like to be a fish feeding on a dead moroccan in the mediterranean. ('I had been wondering', a friend wrote to me three years ago, 'why would I want to bother thinking about, or writing about, or impersonating, a cop, or the Home Office'.) the reading is a total dirge, all black depression and astronomic hopelessness. i hate this right now. the moment it's over I leave and cycle away, i have a headache, i get home, M. has a headache, i feel angry and stamp the anger down, i read a few pages of a scholarly but despairing text about the recent history of Yemen, give up and fall asleep, M. falls asleep, I dream of a desert, of watching a woman give birth, i get up, a Facebook post by my friend R. shows a demo of thousands of Italians on a Calabrian beach, clouds piled up thickly on a metallic blue sky. 'We can win', R. writes: 70 people like this. 'the sea does not want to be infected with leprosy and pus. not yet', writes B Traven, the pseudonymous author of furious disabused novels for anonymous abused people.

***

there is a massive flare up of seborrheic dermatitis on the right hand side of my face. it's the evening of the next day. i'm writing in the historic present tense out of convenience: you'll get used to it. 'i go to' parliament square for the emergency demonstration against the illegal migration bill. the escalator at westminster tube station has a banner ad for a new fighter aircraft designed by BAE: 'delivering **investment** and creating **high skilled jobs** across the UK's regions', the banner was up when i was last here too. when was that? it must have been when i went to the much smaller solidarity vigil for alaa abd el-fattah. today it's 'Commonwealth Day': the flags of Britain's neo-colonial big happy family have been raised around the square, 56 of them running along every side, filtering the bright yellow lights from the church windows, the building of the supreme court, of westminster abbey. that light falls on the thin mud of the 'garden' and makes it look yellow too, like the dirty wet sand on a beach near where the tide is withdrawing. i never noticed before how much this place is enemy territory: i've been here dozens of times but it is always the *event* that i have experienced, never the setting. not deeply. in fact i didn't even realise while i was there that the flags aren't always raised, that they were raised *today*, that 'Commonwealth Day' is *today*, that someone is actually paid to spend their whole working day executing this attempt by state power to carry out a landgrab on calendrical time. i never gave all these symbols any credence, why should i, in a fake socialist regime the flags could be for 'socialist republics' and the statue of winston churchill could be substituted for a big worker in concrete. it would hardly make a difference. and the reason I'm paying attention *now* is just that there's nothing else to pay attention *to*, the defeated MPs of the Labour left are standing outside the building talking about racism, and the victorious MPs of the Labour right are inside talking about 'inefficiency' and 'incompetence', and i am here half-listening to the first group and reading live updates from the speeches of the second on my phone. & this is how the power structure reasserts itself: the spectacle taking place on top of the fire engine in the designated zone of democratic dissent is anticipated and allowed, the few hundred people who have come out to consume it are tolerated, their language of rote though largely sincere moral outrage has been relegated to its proper place, is being articulated and embodied by the people who are professionally expected to articulate it (the head of the FBU is reminding us of the slogans of the International Workingmen's Association – the state has its form of nostalgia, and we have ours), and meanwhile *inside* the building the primary disagreement has become just what it ought to be, a purely formal exchange of opinion about who are the agents best able to implement a programme of national border security *that is itself in no way up for debate*. in circumstances like these, the demo seems to flicker and slide out of focus, i see it as if i'm looking at some kind of bleached diagram, the event and the setting change places, and it is the *constant* thing that i want to describe and not the delusional 'novelty' of the occasion (the 'demo') to which it contributes and gives shape. i wait to cross the road behind richard burgon and diane abbott, wearing their casual suits, going home at the end of another day's work spent opposing the incremental collapse of the system that requires them to do exactly that. i can see burgon's lightweight running shoes. and the air has the first coolness of spring, who cares about this, everyone's played their role, and everyone is waiting for the moment when things really blow up again and no-one's able to act anymore as if this is just how it is.

... i walked out of that poetry reading because the state of depression that it dramatised felt to me like something totally superficial and unreal, like an intoxication, like a pretence. we *want* the destruction of the bridges that connect us to reality, intention to reality, self to world. we want this because once the bridges have been obliterated then no one can object if we go on to indulge ourselves in wild expressions of pain and personal abandonment, which we find comforting. but those connections *aren't* *bridges*, that's such a shitty ready-to-hand metaphor (it's been bludgeoned into me by the news), they're so much finer and subtler than that, even if I find myself walking through a rote demonstration in which everyone is just dutifully playing out their pre-scripted roles (& **obviously** I've played them too) I still have the ability to articulate that reality and to sense it and to reach out to other people who feel the same way: and the haste with which certain people seek to rip through those threads of everyday world-relation and declare them to be phantoms and illusions of the mind is *either* an expression of extreme narcissism or self-loathing or both, and in a way it doesn't matter which, because in the end the result is the same: hubristic declarative unhappiness, backed up by the organs of official reality (it's inevitable uh huh), leading more or less inexorably to actual misery and isolation. i just don't believe in that shit anymore. even the weird angry rash that has spread across my face feels like a kind of relationship to reality as i see and perceive it, and i am bored by the practical respectability attributed by people with more or less the correct socially sanctioned opinions to their own acts of grandstanding demonstrative self-nullification, however much disguised as recognition of the #objective situation#. there is no such thing. and the thought ricochets into the question of what 'accomplishment' in poetry/music etc means, as well as in the 'space' of our politics. the world is *already* designed to rip through the threads of our own meaningful connection to it, and so it is purposeless to go at these threads pre-emptively ourselves. for so long as i am able to talk to people and understand them and make them understand me, i am not going to get depressed about what 'poetry' (also 'politics' etc.) can 'do', or about the supposed fact that too few people are listening to me. poetry and conversation exist on the same level; and everyone who wants more from the former than the latter is as ridiculous as the person who wants a revolution to come to humanity out of the ('objective') world and thinks that the only agency they have is to eradicate the last traces of their own agency. it's day two of commonwealth week: the designated theme is 'Forging a sustainable and peaceful common future'. the worse things get, the more committed i am to defend the threads of my own connection to things and to people. there are bridges that are so thin and so fine that no enemy can follow you across them; and so why flee across them and blow them up? this is all i can manage for today. 'my aim is to express, to the best of my ability, what i feel as an ordinary person'.

(ii) On denial
4 May 2023

Tauola. I. del Lib. II.

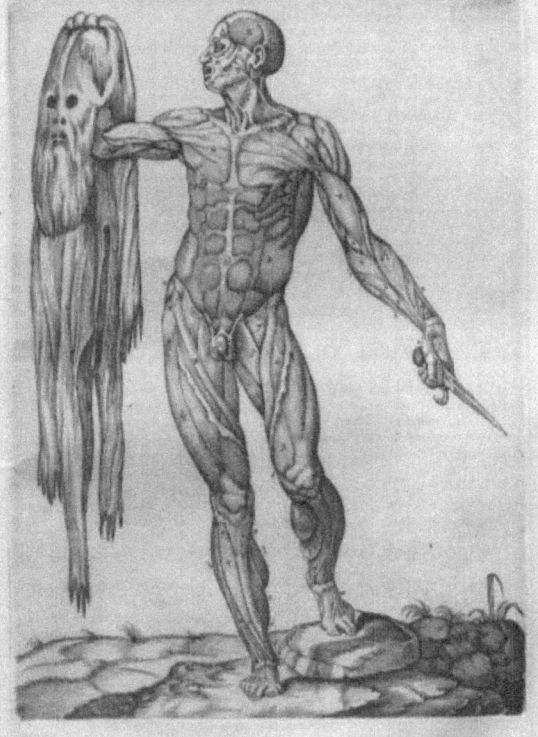

I have been trying to think about my feeling that it is getting harder to talk openly about the things that are happening to us. Does the feeling capture something true? What do I even mean when I say this?

On reflection I think that my 'feeling' stands in for or congeals several related experiences:

1) of a decline, in most of the channels that I can still access (first listservs, now also 'social media') of anything resembling 'political debate' or even extended discussion. These spaces all resemble bars just before closing time -- only the stragglers are left; most of them are talking to themselves etc.;

2) of a more complex disintegration of many underground political and artistic communities. The feeling of people not speaking to one another anymore, or of work that continues, but with less and less sense of common or communal purpose (of course there are countertendencies);

3) connected to (2), a loss of the sense that it is *worth* analysing broad-level political events, a sort of exasperation at the perceived obligation to be *able* to respond to, or to encompass and meaningfully address, the major events of any particular year or week, as the case may be. (The last time I felt a common movement of desire to respond in this way was in the early months of the Covid pandemic. Then responses were filtered into familiar 'pro-' and 'contra' positions and hardened into camps; then silence descended again);

4) more personally, and in a way that makes me distrust my own instincts, I feel a growing impatience with the thinking and the intellectual routines of 'my' culture. On the 'radical left' in particular, the prevailing intellectual 'phase' seems to be one of denial. In relation to Ukraine, I see friends and one-time influences either blatantly cherry-picking facts in order to support their obvious preferred conclusions, or else ignoring the war altogether, because thinking about it is painful and can't be operated upon with our preferred conceptual and practical 'tools'. This experience has produced a kind of paranoia. I find myself wondering how much of my own historical education has been guided by my desire to arrive at pre-determined conclusions. I feel ashamed of what I allowed myself to believe about Kosovo, Lybia, Syria (this also holds when my beliefs were 'agnostic' and not polemical).

A friend writes to me: 'I have a sense that the existence of pro-rationalisers of Putin has been a profound shock to you. I suppose it has not been so much for me, having been so shocked by the British "left" supporting Serbian fascists'.

This was a useful phrase for me. I realised that the existence of 'pro-Putinism' *has* been a shock for me, that it's made me feel as if the ground has been pulled away from under my feet, that I am suddenly suspended in mid-air, that I have nothing to stand on and no base to which to return. It's more than a feeling of 'anger' or 'disappointment', because it is possible to feel angry and disappointed without feeling personally implicated. For the first time in my life, I do feel personally implicated.

I no longer want to defend 'my tradition' against deviations; it is the tradition itself that feels corrupted and untrustworthy. Also the tradition is inside me, and I know neither how much of it is false nor what authority can accurately disclose this

--Something deep inside you sustains a painful injury. You feel instinctively that it might not be fixed anymore. You can't tell yet *how much* is broken: You *know* that something has snapped, but you can't bring yourself to look directly. You still want to believe that it might be 'all in your head', so you continue to look away, and your body fills with adrenaline and this adrenaline is translated into panic or despair or fury directed against those who have betrayed you. But the injury is inside you, and you know that, eventually, you *will* have to look. Something's there.--

I've felt like this now for more than a year. The feeling hasn't abated. I want to look now. 'I know' that in this period 100,000 soldiers have been blown to pieces and millions of people have had to permanently abandon their homes. I know how de rigueur and empty sentences like that have become. I originally wrote 'how fucking empty' but I no longer think empty signifiers of vengeful rage transmit any particular emotional content. 'I yell "Shit" down a cliff at the ocean. Even in my lifetime the immediacy of that word will fade. It will be dead as "Alas."' What I do have is the urge to confess; and I want to understand why it is that it feels so difficult to talk to one another.

***

I wanted to say something about the last time something like this happened. Between 2016 and 2018 we all observed a small group of friends and comrades translate their feelings of exclusion, shame and wounded narcissism into hatred of the 'community' of the radical left. It was a novel spectacle; we gossiped about it and tut tutted. We all knew that the emotional damage *came first* and the post-hoc intellectual apostasy only later. The period 2016-18 provided the perfect stage for this kind of intellectual theatre. But the stage keeps on getting wider and wider, and I'm not sure who is in the audience anymore.

***

What does it feel like to look at an incurable wound? I realise that I'm returning to two distinct metaphors here. I realise that my thinking is incomplete and liable to be misunderstood for that reason. I started this 'project' (this 'blog') because I wanted to try to create a space where we could talk about undecided and unsettled things in a language that is itself unsettled and undecided. I now know that that itself requires an expenditure of effort and sensitivity of which I am not always capable. I *feel* undecided. I also know how easy it is to say things that I don't mean, or that mean more than I mean to mean. And I know about opportunists and renegades and apostates.

The first of the two metaphors I recur to is the metaphor of an outside. The emotionally damaged ex-leftists of 2016-18 talked about stepping outside all the time; they were obsessed with it, the language recurred like a leitmotiv in their writing, like a pole star; it was inescapable, it was almost poetic:

--Something deep inside you sustains an painful injury. You *know* that something has snapped, but you can't bear to look at it directly. And you still want to believe that it might be 'all in your head', so you continue to look away, and your body fills with adrenaline and this adrenaline is translated into panic or sadness or fury directed against those who have betrayed you. But the injury is inside you, so you know that, eventually, you *will* have to look. Something's there.--

but there is no outside to an injury. That's the whole reason why you're not able to look. You know that whatever you see, once you've seen it, will be a part of you, that it will *be* you, for as long as you continue to live: and all you can do is accept that internal reality or deny it, retreating deeper and deeper into a kind of hallucination, a beautiful dream, in which everything's OK and still pristine, and just like it originally was, undamaged, brand new, like a new toy, or a theory that has just opened your eyes. *Looking* means accepting that the wound is there, that it changes everything and that possibility for you will from now on have to be defined through the parameters that it establishes. *Not looking* means holding on to the possibility of the outside (of exteriority of injury to self) in its attenuated form as a kind of feverish denial: a dream valediction. Which do you choose? What can we do with this limb, this hour, this remnant, this fucked up tradition full of emotionally damaged people, this demi-language, etc.? And what is a theory of political action for someone who is (or equally, for a class of people who are) tortured, hunted, imprisoned, injured, or aphasic? Revolutionaries don't like to think about this, the preestablished outputs invalidate the inputs. The problem is relegated to 'poetry' and poetry regurgitates its usual reservoirs of generic panic and despair. How tasteless. Which metaphor do you prefer?

> That one must sacrifice coherence
> to the incoherence of life, attempt a creator
> dialogue, even if that goes against our conscience.
>
> That the reality of this small, stingy state
> is greater than us, is always an awesome thing
> and one must be a part of it, however bitter that is.[58]

*

I still don't think I'm putting any of this right. I'll post it anyway. Perhaps someone can correct me. What does Pasolini mean by 'creator / dialogue'? What does he mean by 'against our conscience'? What does he mean by 'our'? What does he mean by 'be a part of it'? What does he mean?

(iii) Letter to Danny by William Rowe
14 May 2023

Dear Danny,

I address this to you as open dialogue. I want to reply to your recent piece in Reports. The title you give it is 'On Denial', a word with strong resonance in current time. I mean that denial has become that kind of word for me, and I will try to say why.

There's a subjective satisfaction in the act of denial. The one who says 'it never happened' invokes a certain power—like saying X didn't happen, or not in the way 'you say it happened'—the X could be Grenfell Tower, the event of it covered by a mass of legal procedure that wraps itself around justice; the 'you' being those who were burnt to death, or the voice that has to speak for them. That's a case of implicit denial, the subjects being the companies that issued the cladding materials, the local council, the government, the majority of the media.

Inside the self, we know that denial manages to put something else in the place of damage suffered, something that can cover it while also perpetuating it. But there's another kind of denial also, which doesn't respond to knowing, since it expunges, removes the very space in which a thing has occurred or is occurring. This is not to say that the damage-event that's denied is inexpressible; Fran Lock calls it horseflesh. But such forms of expression are strictly non-exchangeable. They are thought-figures which are forbidden to drift above themselves and be creamed off. Not allowing a thought-figure to drift into the sphere of exchange is a principle that gets laid down at the beginning of your poem *Loading Terminal*.

It's very hard not to slide into some kind of denial inside the intractability of current crises—political, ecological but also crises of language and thought. Language exhausts itself quickly. I think I mean language in its function of 'is', of predication, of naming.

Freud's notion of 'binding' came into the conversation at the recent MayDay Rooms meeting. Freud's use of the term, where binding works in terms of 'an energy which flows along chains of ideas and implies associative "links"', suggests a possible cross-over between inner life and the political outside. When you write 'there is no outside to an injury' are you posing this as an outside where resolution might have been possible? I want to say that a wound with no outside is the pair of a situation with no solution—a situation where words are stuck in chains of association that perpetuate an impasse. Not that individual wound and social wound are homologous, but that they exist in a certain relation to each other. What kind of relation? The insistent trauma-talk of narcissistic selves falsifies the relation. Once you accept that life is suffering, you can accept the challenge of living. That's Jordan Peterson speaking, and inside his voice the long history of voices that have said that suffering is an entirely internal matter, a belief highly acceptable to capitalism. Individual wound and social wound are not homologous but what they have in common is isolation.

Rimbaud's poem 'The Drunken Boat' sums up a basic element of Leftist tradition: to break all moorings, the call to rebellion as radical subjective unbinding, the legacy of the Paris Commune gathered into that call, that cell of meaning. That Rimbaud got labelled a *poète maudit* was a manoeuvre of bourgeois literature, we know that. The boat lands in Africa and finds itself facing white men with firearms: subjective emancipation includes colonial violence. That's the corrective to individualism. But the binding, undone, without new binding consisting of a changed social order—does it go where we need to go? Does it merely end up bending to a new master?

That seems to be more a question for those, like myself, who experienced 1968. 'All things come into their comparisons', Robert Duncan wrote in the nineteen sixties. Now everything seems to face its limit: not just emancipatory politics but ideas of the commons and the collective and of political will as such.

I'm not arguing for the abandonment of that tradition (you refer to people who have done that) but that our account of where we are should acknowledge the unmooring of ideas from their historical basis, right down to the linkage of words in their phrasing. I'm reminded of the slogan that headed an announcement of the recent International Workers' Memorial Day. It said 'Mourn for the dead. Fight for the living.' It might have been better the other way round; then there wouldn't have been the illusion of a place to fight from.

So, to mark some conditions that determine our situation: wars in Europe and the middle east; resurgence of oil and arms industries; postponement of any real, state-level action to resolve climate crisis; inability of states and ruling classes to guarantee survival; political chaos. These add up to time for new analysis, critique of inherited models for revolution—critique, for instance, of the thinking that assumed that the Soviet revolution constituted a necessary pathway for struggles in other places (but also critique of flat rejection of the Bolshevik experience), as well as critique of capitalist subjectivation in ourselves, including the production of isolation. I was going to write 'the production of isolation and confusion', but attributing confusion simply to action of the political enemy seems one-sided. A least, I sense that a future MDR discussion of confusion might have to take that on.

(iv) Response to William Rowe ['On Denial']
25 May 2023

Dear Will,

Thank you for responding, for opening this up into a conversation. I think you're right to push us back towards things that are actually happening: the 'conditions which determine our situation'. Those are the hardest things to talk about, but I'll try at least to follow you in their direction.

...

Towards the end of your letter you talk about Rimbaud's unbinding as a 'basic element of Leftist tradition: to break all moorings'. You also say that we presently *feel* unmoored, that this unmooring is the default, and that we 'should acknowledge the unmooring of ideas from their historical basis, right down to the linkage of words in their phrasing'. This recalls to my mind Stephen Hastings-King's metaphor in the text we discussed in our first MayDay Rooms meeting: 'we float', SH-K wrote, 'like plankton ... near the surface of an online sea'.[59] And so unmooring itself becomes unmoored, is no longer a call to rebellion as radical subjective unbinding. And the unmooring that seems nearest to us is not the unmooring we know from Rimbaud but the one that was immortalised in Mayakovsky's suicide poem (in which 'the love boat has smashed against convention'), or the devastatingly prosaic unmooring of tiny isolated floating organisms which serve as food for larger and more complex systems. Capital, for example.

Plankton, meaning to drift, or wander in a sea.

So, is this part of what at the end of your letter you call 'confusion': that we no longer know what it means to 'rebel'? The mark made on our intellectual lives by years of fascist provocation is obviously relevant here, but there are other things at stake too. In the first draft of the reply I wrote to you, I finished by saying that 'for a long time I've felt really sick, and now I feel less so, and I want to try to talk about why'. I've been thinking a lot recently about Ernst Bloch's *The Principle of Hope*, this giant luminescent encyclopaedia of images of the other world scattered through human history in fairytales and myths and scientific theories and music. Yesterday when I first tried to get down my response, I made an attempt to talk about this 'hope' in terms of space, and poetry. I wrote about Satan's passage through chaos in *Paradise Lost*, and Pasolini's 'Testimony' in which he describes walking 'all night long' through filthy suburbs in search of sex ('the sex is a pretext', he says), and about Alice Rahon, who says that 'for a while now, I've lived inside a map on the wall'. And that wasn't wrong, exactly, but the emphasis isn't in the right place. What I want to describe to you is a *feeling that there isn't space anymore*, that there isn't space for us to think, that all of the available positions have been occupied already by something foul and that wherever we go we find ourselves in the same cramped room, surrounded by our enemies. And when in your email you point out to me that grifting conservative psychologists also instruct us 'to accept the challenge of life' (as, in one of my proselytising moods, I might also have done) I feel a trace of this claustrophobia rise up in me again, a thin sheet of panic that has been working its way through my body for years now, and which acquires another layer every time I try to think about what 'radical politics' is: and always there's this sense that I'm standing in the middle of a room surrounded by people who I can't bear, and if I try to move away from one person I move closer to another, and the doors on either side of the room are marked 'acceptance' and 'denial', and both lead into another identical room where the same problem is repeated.

I said earlier that I want personal pain to be undignified, that I want to accept (not to *deny*) that political concepts will cover it badly, that I want to accept that the pain will stick out or bulge in ways that seem unseemly or gross or ridiculous. I said that I want to find that fucking funny and for the comedy to be as it were 'communally recognised', and not a grounds for personal affront or retreat into vast vanilla terrain (a green area?)[60] of aristocratic interior self-regard, disdain for mass politics, educated immunity to illusion etc. 'For a long time I've felt really sick, and now I feel less so, and I want to try to talk about why'. And clearly this is a thought about how things fit together or don't, and about what it means to talk about 'coherence', or 'cohesiveness'. Along with the Bloch I've been reflecting on the way Pasolini could say the most reactionary things *and yet expect them to mean something different to what they seemed to mean*, because poetry in his conception opens up into the unexpected space inside of our own bodies and in political parties and suburbs and the ideas of reactionaries and teenage boys as well as Communists and mothers and lovers and streets, because he still knew how to rebel, or maybe just because he wasn't afflicted by this mindless claustrophobia like us, which we only call 'confusion' because we've forgotten that there is something that needs to be done *beyond organising concepts in their relations to each another,* and because we no longer see that the more organised these concepts become *the more 'confused' we tend to be*, because each of them becomes more and more like a point on a grid or a node in a system of coordinates that have no internal dimensions and no field of possibilities and so no fucking principle of hope either. And we are trapped inside of those points, feeling claustrophobic and confused, wondering whether we should have started another one of those nice abstract conversations about feelings. THERE IS NO OUTSIDE TO INJURY, I write, thoughtfully.

So at least now we have a list of terms. Incoherence, confusion – and claustrophobia. I'm tempted to say that we also have a list of counter-terms (coherence, lucidity, ability to move), but that feels too convenient and anyway like I say excessive 'coherence' is *an aspect* of claustrophobia and not its antidote. Rather I think the point should be about finding a way to move backwards through the sequence, from claustrophobia through confusion and back out again into the 'incoherence of life' where space opens up inside of things unexpectedly and it's a part of our (one might call it) 'intellectual training' *to prepare ourselves* -- meaning, to make sure we're ready when it happens.
...

And can I try to lever a question out of all this. Is it possible to talk, Will, about the very large things that you mention at the end of your letter -- 'wars in Europe and the middle east; resurgence of oil and arms industries; postponement of any real, state-level action to resolve climate crisis; inability of states and ruling classes to guarantee survival; political chaos' -- or to oppose them -- without feeling like *they are themselves* the walls that are closing in, the answers that have been poured like concrete into their questions, the wall of convention that Mayakovsky's love boat smashes into? If I feel less mentally 'sick' now than I did (and if I keep repeating this it's because I want to convince myself that it's true), it's because I've stopped screaming at myself. I have stopped telling myself to piece things together. I am trying to meet things differently, to ask different questions of them. I don't ask them to behave like keys. Does this make sense? 'To know how to recognise and pick up the signs of power we are awaiting, which are everywhere' (Tristan Tzara) -- and specifically Tzara says *to pick them up*, like radio signals in the air, rather than to bend them out of shape *like* picks for a self-invented lock in a single self-imposed theoretical door. I know this must sound stupidly obvious. But it is a principle of hope for me.

(v) One More Time On Damage
9 June 2023

the other city was beautiful: the sky was completely cloudless and the street demonstration was larger and full of red smoke. grass is greener etc. i still felt frustrated, like i always do, that the things that i want to say i can never put right, that the 'stakes' never come across clearly, that i am continually allowing my arguments to be derailed by the minor satisfactions of the crescendo, the hissy fit or rhetorical blowout, tilting at windmills, trying to show off, making a verbal scene. i felt dismayed that the response that i wrote to Will had veered off into a display of over-inflated egoistic disappointment that might have felt to him like an attack, when i felt nothing but gratitude to him for the way of his thinking and for the other paths that his thoughts had opened up. i was reading anna mendelssohn's *Implacable Art*, which once again seemed to demonstrate to me something fundamental that i have felt and have wanted to get across.

a few related thoughts have been at the centre of everything that i have recently written. so the following as a kind of abstract (and perhaps also as a provisional full stop):

(i) i have been trying to articulate for myself the idea of a communist resilience that we can develop in ourselves, a way of being; and along with that comes the longing for a style and a form of thought and a way of speaking in which that mode of being can be expressed implicitly and at every turn, regardless of the particular thing that happens to be being said, or articulated. if we could cultivate that style, i sometimes think, then it would be possible to talk about how to stay alive, how not to abandon ourselves to unhappiness, how to live well alongside one another, how not to get isolated, without those things becoming their own self-sufficient horizons and replacing 'politics' (or class struggle) as the ultimate object of our concern. we would speak more openly and freely, without internalised guilt for addressing the 'wrong' subjects, or abandoning our earlier commitments, and we would be secure in the knowledge that our style and our way of speech (and perhaps finally just *who we are*) would guarantee the connection of our thinking to ultimate ends -- commitments that we no longer even need to name, or identify, or conceptualise, because they are just there in the *way* that we speak, and live. and so we would be liberated from the hateful gut-wrenching sensation of confusion that comes from watching our friends and comrades start to say things that are foul to us, using the language (but not the style) that we too have invested our lives in, and fought for and attempted to define. we would cease to feel as if we were trapped in a kind of labyrinth, in which by following our 'ideas' to their logical conclusions we travel further and further away from the principles that initially motivated them. 'and so / I am only interested in nonexploitative relations between people // the people who sneer at that 'on our side' are not on our side / our side is the people who do not sneer like that / and there are no others sides // only illusions mirages and labyrinths of words / that lead us away from ourselves'. just before i left i saw a friend who said he was only interested in tyrannicide, something else that i forget, and modern art. and i recognise this impulse immediately: to retreat to basic principles, to want to find ways not to get lost, to screen out the noise and the confusion and the distractions and the smokescreens and the people who don't interest us. and all of us are going through this same process in different ways, and we are only just beginning to share with one another our thoughts about what it is that we need to do. i want to know what more of my friends have thought to themselves about this problem, to see how it is processed through their own vocabularies and terms of reference. i can feel very painfully the limits of my own.

(ii) *and too many of us have been playing roles in an elite-class game. the system of elite-class writing in its current phase makes a virtue of injury: the speaking subject should be injured. the injury should come from a marginal position, whether of race or class or gender or migration. representation of the group injury as personal experience (= as property) is a condition of entry into the elite class system of representation in the current phase of its management of group injuries that it presides over and inflicts. the representation-game i am talking about increases the resilience of that system, and turns ramifying collective losses to its own spectacular advantage. it has been hegemonic in the 'cultural sphere' in roughly the period 2013 to today, which means: in more or less the same period in which global economic crisis was remedied by means of mass economic austerities and bureaucratic state violence. (but i'm not pointing fingers. we've all played it.)*

(iii) that's a specimen of 'analysis'. the person who i was thinking of when i wrote it is dead now, which means that it probably isn't sufficient... 'the communist party is not a big clean party', wrote p-p pasolini, 'it is a big dirty party;

but it is dirty with the oil of the shop, with metal, with rust, flour, dried fish, blood, mint, sweat, and dust'. and sometimes i think what we really need is a canon. writers who have tried to bring their ideas closer to damaged and injured ('dirty') people (including themselves) include andrei platonov, pasolini, ivan illich, anna mendelssohn, m. e. o'brien ('junkie communism'), verity spott ('that horrible burning religion') and william blake. the 'dirty party', the idea of revolutionary harm reduction, of convivial technology, of the marriage of heaven and hell -- all of these notions point towards a style of thinking in which grand revolutionary transformation belongs to the damaged and resembles them, *rather than vice versa*, and in which damage and injury are *inescapable starting points* and not moral virtues for their own sake: the goal then is still emphatically to create the new social order, but one that the damaged and the injured *in this world* are themselves able to control and comprehend. there are snatches of romanian and polish in it, of bengali and salt-sea, incense and fishblood and weed smoke in arcades: obviously it all depends on exactly where you come from. but there are also other things as well: arguments, visions, utopias. the thing that we want does not come solely from the future. it does not gleam. it is not at the cutting edge.

(iv) the emergence of an elite class game of injury-representation does not reduce or ameliorate group injury, but is continuous with the processes that inflict it in the first place: ok sure, but also *the lucid recognition of this reality is not enough to help us to endure*. the people who taught me to recognise it themselves seem pretty fucked up right now, have become confused, isolated or cut off, unable to situate themselves in the present in which the ideas they once articulated are taken up by the mass culture and twisted spitefully against them. it seems really obvious to me that they lack the resources to survive, and i think now that part of the problem is that *they didn't develop a style*, a way of being that would allow them to go after those resources *without feeling that they were abandoning their basic conviction: that everything had to change before their own condition did, or could, or might*. 'we play our lives like pieces of music', somebody writes. 'We know that a perfect score exists, but we can't read it; and the hesitant discordant melody that we do execute is in the end the only access we have to the music of our lives as we know that it really is'.

(iv) i think that probably most of us who love poetry have the conviction that there is one bit or snatch or line of it that seems to define everything else and to encompass it: a kind of ur-poetry, possessing an almost metaphysical significance. for me those lines have always been the ones from william blake's 'london': '[i] mark in every face i meet / marks of weakness, marks of woe'. and i mean it. i come back to those words every single day, like a mantra. they encapsulate for me the task of poetry and a basic challenge to 'my' politics, to my belief that things can change, that they don't have to be like this. and the struggle as i have felt it has always been to understand *in what sense the lines can be true*, in what sense the 'marks' (which i have always felt must be *indelible*) can be real, without the belief that things can change being proved false, or illusory; and it's only pretty recently that i've begun to feel as if i have a way of answering that question. try it like this. imagine a universe in which these lines of blake's are the centre and project outwards invisible fields of force, invisible lines of gravity within which everything else is located: 'the class struggle', economic reforms, principles of hope, going to work, reading the news, producing art, 'reproducing yourself'. and we don't 'talk' about these fields, but everything that we *do* talk about moves within them insensibly: pasolini's rust and fish and dried blood and smoke in the air and our ideas about 'communism' all move within this forcefield that blake's lines define, and delineate. so the point is that when these marks of weakness, marks of woe are thought or felt like this *they don't rule anything else out*, the fact of their irremediability does not rule out revolution or happiness or, i don't know, whatever you like, transcendence, renewal, jfc even spiritual insight if you want it, they just don't, and the borders and walls and inner citadels of 'real injury' outside of which everything else is just pipe dreams and adolescent fantasies crumble like 'Cathedrals ... based on symmetry which later becomes magmatic, abnormal and out of proportion'. *nothing is ruled out, nothing is destroyed, nothing left behind*, we play the notes of our life in the wrong order, and somehow we still hear the music as it really is, even though it can only ever exist like this, in the way that we're playing it right now: misphrased, discordant, a little slow, a little hesitant. and everything is the same and everything is different, and we are travelling backwards in time towards a thing that no one has ever seen before: and when i started writing these notes a few months ago i wanted to talk about what had gone wrong, i had the feeling that so many of us had lost our way, that the damage was accumulating but that we didn't know how to get it into words (I don't mean with 'professionals'), that even the act of opening our mouths to talk about ourselves would fill us with unwanted invasive feelings of guilt, and now it's six months later and i'm starting to feel like i've turned a corner, as if i've finally understood something basic and something has clicked or become clear: that blake's universe of woe and weakness is really just a set of rules, as indifferent and as mild and as neutral as electromagnetism, or gravity, or multiplication, and it is only when it ceases to be the substance of our style and our way of being that it becomes unbearable and stops us from thinking; but when it exists in our style or way of being everything else becomes possible again, we can go back to our political ideas and see them in a new light, changed but also persistent, and enduring, and for the first time in our life maybe they really seem like *our* ideas too, like things which are coming towards *us*, as the planets move towards the objects at the centre of their orbits; and maybe this feels good? to no longer have to chase after *them*, feeling ourselves getting weaker and weaker, and less and less able to remember why it is that we started, and looking up sometimes and seeing them always further and further away? i don't know, you tell me. we all know that when a new chapter of our lives begins, it'll have to be lived day by day: and there are notes that none of us have been able to play, and we hear them anyway in the notes that we are able to play, and do. perhaps even here.

Endnotes

1   Keston Sutherland, 'Diplomatica Fides', *Poetical Works, 1999–2015* (London: Enitharmon, 2015), p. 128.

2   Johan Huizinga, *Homo Ludens: A Study of the Play-Element in Culture* (London: Routledge, 1949), p. 119.

3   *Get Rid of Yourself* is available in full at: https://www.youtube.com/watch?v=CyMUt8cBRsg&t=2619s&ab_channel=RevolutionaryAudiobooks. A transcript is available at: https://anarchistwithoutcontent.wordpress.com/2011/07/04/get-rid-of-yourself-transcript/.

4   Huizinga, *Homo Ludens*, p. 134.

5   Ibid.

6   Emmanuel Le Roy Ladurie, *Carnival in Romans: People's Uprising at Romans, 1579 –1580*, trans. Mary Feeney (London: Scholar Books, 1979), p. 182.

7   https://dojo.tech/blog/uk-cash-machine-declines/

8   https://en.wikipedia.org/wiki/Automated_teller_machine

9   I'm not particularly interested in Bernadette Corporation and that's not what this is about, but some background on the 'it-girl'/post-situ context for anyone curious is Jian-Xing Too, 'Burn a Debt to the Present', *Afterall: A Journal of Art, Context, and Enquiry*, 14 (Autumn/Winter 2006): 62–70. See also note xxvii.

10   Huizinga, *Homo Ludens*, p. 12.

11   LeRoi Jones [Amiri Baraka], *Blues People: Negro Experience in White America* (New York: William Morrow, 1963), p. 68.

12   The most famous modern presentation of this theory is Victor Turner, *The Forest of Symbols: Aspects of Ndembu Ritual* (Ithaca, NY: Cornell University Press, 1967).

13   Sandra Billington, *Social History of the Fool* (Sussex: The Harvester Press, 1984), p. 17.

14   'It was, perhaps, the confidence de Cusa placed in his own philosophical work, *Coincidentia Oppositorum*, and not theology which led to the secular tone. The philosophy was based on a mathematical hypothesis that the greatest cannot be greater not less, else it would not be the greatest; and the least cannot be greater nor less, else it would not be least. Therefore, the greatest and least are equal, and, by extension, the Fool can represent God' (Billington, *A Social History of the Fool*, p. 24).

15   Friedrich Schiller, *On the Naïve and Sentimental in Literature*, trans. Helen Watanabe-O'Kelly (Manchester: Carcanet, 1981, p. 59). O'Kelly uses 'suspended' for 'aufhebt'. The full passage is 'Aber eben das macht ja den Dichter aus, daß er alles in sich aufhebt, was an eine künstliche Welt erinnert, daß er die Natur in ihrer ursprünglichen Einfalt wieder in sich herzustellen weiß. Hat er aber dieses gethan, so ist er auch eben dadurch von allen Gesetzen losgesprochen, durch die ein verführtes Herz sich gegen sich selbst sicher stellt. Er ist rein, er ist unschuldig, und was der unschuldigen Natur erlaubt ist, ist es auch ihm; bist du, der du ihn liesest oder hörst, nicht mehr schuldlos, und kannst du es nicht einmal momentweise durch seine reinigende Gegenwart werden, so ist es dein Unglück und nicht das seine; du verlässest ihn, er hat für dich nicht gesungen'. There are good reasons for 'suspended': Schiller talks in legal terms

('he is acquitted from all laws'), and in this context a law is more likely to be 'suspended' than 'annulled'. But the context is a discussion of the poet knowing to produce in himself nature in its original simplicity – if *fabricating* (herstellen) is the metaphor, and 'simplicity' is what is being produced, then annulment and purgation rather than suspension would seem to be the active sense of this instance of the verb aufheben. The likely scenario of course is that Schiller was dimly aware of both metaphorical 'scenes'.

16   I am quoting from the early version reproduced on Donna Fleischer's blog *word pond*: https://donnafleischer.wordpress.com/2015/08/15/lazy-eye-haver-sandra/. A version of the poem published later in Reines' *A Sand Book* deletes both the stanza with the dashcam and the closing lines on the 'language purge'. I prefer the version in which the language purge was still being proposed to the version from which the purge is purged. See Ariana Reines, *The Sand Book* (Portland, OR: Tin House Books, 2020).

17   June Jordan, *On Call: Political Essays* (Boston, MA: South End Press, 1985), p. 14.

18   Sean Bonney, *Our Death* (Oakland, CA: Commune Editions, 2019), p. 61.

19   Paul Celan, *Selected Poems*, trans. Michael Hamburger (London: Penguin, 1996), 141. 'Lies nicht mehr – schau! Schau nicht mehr – geh!'

20   Situationist International, 'Decline and Fall of the Spectacle Economy', http://www.bopsecrets.org/SI/10.Watts.htm.

21   André Jolles, *Simple Forms*, trans. Peter J. Schwartz (London: Verso, 2017), Chapter 4, The Riddle,

'VIII. The Mental Disposition Of Knowledge – Examples – The Rune'.

22   Ibid., Chapter 4, The Riddle, 'IV. Reasons For Riddling – Initiation and *"Bund"* or Association'.

23   Ibid., Chapter 4, The Riddle, 'VII. Special Language and Riddle Form – Double Solution'.

24   Karl Marx, *Economic and Philosophic Manuscripts of 1844*, https://www.marxists.org/archive/marx/works/1844/manuscripts/comm.htm.

25   Karl Marx, Preface to *A Contribution to the Critique of Political Economy*: 'Mankind thus inevitably sets itself only such tasks as it is able to solve, since closer examination will always show that the problem itself arises only when the material conditions for its solution are already present or at least in the course of formation'. https://www.marxists.org/archive/marx/works/1859/critique-pol-economy/preface.htm.

26   Jolles, *Simple Forms*, Chapter 4, The Riddle, 'VII. Special Language and Riddle Form – Double Solution'.

27   Bernadette Corporation lean heavily on the concepts (and I assumed the actual writing, whether detourned or commissioned) of Tiqqun/The Invisible Committee, whose *Preliminary Materials for a Theory of the Young-Girl* was translated for Semiotext(e) by Ariana Reines. Tiqqun, *Preliminary Materials for a Theory of the Young-Girl*, trans. Ariana Reines (New York: Semiotext(e), 2012).

28   Heinrich Heine, *Über Ludwig Börne*, https://www.projekt-gutenberg.org/heine/boerne/index.html. My translation.

29   Paul Celan, 'The Meridian', *Collected Prose*, trans. Rosemary Waldrop (New York: Routledge, 2003),

p. 37.

30   Dom Hale, Seizures (Leeds: Gong Farm, 2022); Tom Crompton, Definitions (Leeds: Gong Farm, 2022).

31   The Poets' Hardship Fund is a poetry mutual aid project started in the wake of the various mutual aid activities that sprang up and died away during the period of the Covid lockdowns in 2020. It collects money via donations for a monthly magazine, *Ludd Gang*, and disburses no-questions-asked payments of £50 to poets in need: https://poetshardshipfunduk.com/.

32   The Poets' Hardship Fund, *Ill Pips* (Leeds, Edinburgh, London: Gong Farm, 2022).

33   Elsa Dorling, *Self-Defense: A Philosophy of Violence*, trans. Kieran Aarons (London: Verso, 2022), p. 58.

34   Georg Büchner, *Complete Works and Letters*, ed. Walter Hinderer (New York: Continuum, 1976).

35   Anne Boyer, *A Handbook of Disappointed Fate* (New York: Ugly Duckling Presse, 2018).

36   'Distance, Einstein said, goes around in circles. This | Is the opposite of a party or a social gathering. | It does not give much distance to go on'. Jack Spicer, *My Vocabulary Did This to Me: The Collected Poetry of Jack Spicer*, eds. Kevin Killian and Peter Gizzi (Middleton, CT: Wesleyan University Press, 2008), p. 384.

37   Ibid., p. 382. 'The baseball season finished. The | Bumble-bee there cruising over a few poor flowers. | They have cut the ground from under us. The touch | Of your hands on my back. The Giants | Winning 93 games | Is as impossible | In spirit | As the grass we might walk on'.

38   Percy Bysshe Shelley, 'A Defence of Poetry', in *The Selected Prose Works of Shelley*, ed. Henry S. Salt (London: Watts & Co., 1915), p. 117.

39   Spicer, *My Language Did This to Me:* 'The ground still squirming. The ground still not fixed as I | thought it would be in an adult world. | Sandy growls like a wolf. The space between him and his image | is greater than the space between me and my image' (p. 383).

40   For the quotation, taken from Jakobson's still untranslated *O cesskom stixe*, see Victor Erlich, *Russian Formalism: History-Doctrine* (The Hague: Mouton, 1969), p. 219. The assumption that Jakobson was talking about 'literature' seems to derive from a truncated quotation of Erlich's quotation at the beginning of Terry Eagleton's *Literary Theory: An Introduction.*

41   Ivan Illich, *Tools for Conviviality* (New York: Fontana, 1971), p. 31. Illich's writings seem to me useful for thinking about poetry, which itself obviously both is and is not a tool.

42   Diane di Prima, *Revolutionary Letters* (San Francisco, CA: Last Gasp, 2005), p. 8. we die | a million times a day, | we are born | a million times, each breath life and death: | get up, put on your shoes, get | started, someone will finish'.

43   This is a version of an imperative first formulated by Mayakovsky (or perhaps by Whitman): 'In the name of raising the qualifications of poets, in the name of the future blossoming of poetry, we must expunge the idea that such facile undertakings should stand apart from other aspects of human endeavour' ('How are Verses Made', p. 45). Spicer's remarks were made in his first 'Vancouver Lecture': 'But what you want to say – the

business of the wanting coming from Outside, like it wants five dollars being ten dollars, that kind of want – is the real thing, the thing that you didn't *want* to say in terms of your own ego, in terms of your image, in terms of your life, in terms of everything'. *The House that Jack Built: The Collected Lectures of Jack Spicer*, ed. Peter Gizzi (Middleton, CT: Wesleyan University Press, 1998), p. 6. Peter Gizzi rightly says that this places the poet 'in the frankly clerical position of a fatigued copyist, or, at most, a translator' (p. 50).

44   See Pierre Bourdieu et al., *Photography: A Middle-brow Art*, trans. Shaun Whiteside (Oxford: Polity Press, 1990). The French title is *Un art moyen*. 'Most of society can be excluded from the universe of legitimate culture without being excluded from the universe of aesthetics', says Pierre Bourdieu. 'There are beautiful ways of trimming a hedge'.

45   Hölderlin, 'Der Rhein': 'Denn weil | Die Seligsten nichts fühlen von selbst, | Muß wohl, wenn solches zu sagen | Erlaubt ist, in der Götter Namen | Teilnehmend fühlen ein andrer'. The poem is available in facing translation at https://sites.google.com/site/germanliterature/19th-century/hoelderlin/der-rhein-the-rhine.

46   https://dreamcrusher.bandcamp.com/track/another-country. The title, I realised later, is taken from James Baldwin. But it means more to me as the title of a piece of music.

47   Dom Hale, 'Asbestosis', unpublished. 'that I look up for a sec | at this huge green nameless tree | breathing pretty quiet overhead, bracelet of | wind stranded by the edge of the road | where no one's famous | & absolutely

everything could be stolen back'.

48   Fanny Howe, *London-Rose: Beauty Will Save the World* (Brussels: Divided Press, 2022), p. 62.

49   Pierre Paolo Pasolini, 'A Desperate Vitality', in *The Selected Poetry of Pier Paolo Pasolini*, p. 351. '(Ah, I'm using a generic plural, you see: Them! | with the madman's complicitous love of his illness.)' Pasolini also writes 'However | (write! write!) my present | confusion is the result | of a Fascist victory' (p. 351).

50   Charles Baudelaire, *The Essence of Laughter, and other essays, journals and letters*, ed. Peter Quennell (New York: Meridian, 1956), p. 106.

51   Evgenia Belorusets, *Modern Animal*, trans. Bela Shayevich (Italy: Common Era, 2021), p. 138.

52   Carl Jung, *The Collected Works of C. G. Jung*, vol. 5, *Symbols of Transformation*, trans. R. F. C. Hull (London: Routledge, 1956), p. 233.

53   Walt Whitman, *Song of Myself: With a Complete Commentary* (Iowa City: University of Iowa Press, 2016), p. 67. Cited in Jordan's *On Call: Political Essays*.

54   J. H. Prynne, 'L'Extase de M. Poher', *Poems* (Newcastle upon Tyne: Bloodaxe, 1999), p. 162. Rubbish is 'the | ultimate sexual point of the whole place turned | into a model question'.

55   Sarah Brouillette, 'The Consolations of Heterosexual Monogamy in Sally Rooney's Beautiful World, Where Are You', *Blindfield Journal*, https://blindfieldjournal.com/2021/09/30/the-consolations-of-heterosexual-monogomy-in-sally-rooneys-beautiful-world-where-are-you/.

56   Banu, Introduction to Leijia Hanrahan,

'Communism Won't Save Us From Ourselves', *Ill-Will*, https://illwill.com/communism-wont-save-us-from-ourselves.

57   The following texts, four by me and one by William Rowe, originated in a series of discussions of poetry and politics that took place at MayDay Rooms in London between February and July 2023, hence occasional references to 'meetings'. Some minutes from these discussions, as well as lists of texts discussed, were published on the 'Reports' blog at www.communityofgoods.blogspit.com.

58   Pierre Paolo Pasolini, 'Victory', translated by Norman MacAfee, https://znetwork.org/znetarticle/victory-by-pier-paolo-pasolini/. The lines quoted are in fact a ventriloquism of Pietro Nenni, post-war leader of the Italian Socialist Party; but I don't see that it's important whether Pasolini 'meant' them or not.

59   Stephen Hastings-King, 'Parallax: Four Perspectives on Russia', 6 April 2022: https://aljumhuriya.net/en/2022/04/06/parallax-four-perspectives-on-russia/.

60   William translated 'Green Areas', a section of Raúl Zurita's *Purgatory*. We discussed this text in the Reports 'series' on 17 April.

Danny Hayward's most recent poetry collection is *Loading Terminal* (87 Press, 2022). More recent work, along with an earlier collection of critical essays, can be accessed at Free Trials <www.pxxtry.com>

Copyright © remains with the author.
Writing from Dom Hale and William Rowe
by kind permission of the authors.

978-1-915000-01-9

Inner book template, cover design template,
and logo by Robbie Dawson.

Brighton
2024

www.ingramcontent.com/pod-product-compliance
Lightning Source LLC
Chambersburg PA
CBHW020132130526
44590CB00040B/559